No Backbone!
The World of Invertebrates

Creeping Land Snails

by Nancy White

Consultant: Lindsey T. Groves
Collection Manager, Malacology Section
Natural History Museum of Los Angeles County

BEARPORT
PUBLISHING

NEW YORK, NEW YORK

Credits

Cover, © B. Marielle and © Magdalena Bujak/Shutterstock; TOC, © Andrea Haase/Shutterstock; 4-5, © Michael Lander/Nordic Photos/Photolibrary; 6, © Alan Henderson; 7, © Alan Henderson; 9, © Panorama Stock/Photolibrary; 10, © Mawroidis Kamila/Shutterstock; 11, © ANT Photo Library/Photo Researchers, Inc.; 12, © Alan Henderson; 13, © Robert Maier/Animals Animals Earth Scenes/Photolibrary; 14, © John Cancalosi/Photolibrary; 15, © Gary Meszaros/Visuals Unlimited; 16-17, © Gary K. Smith/Nature Picture Library; 18, © Martin Brigdale/Fresh Food Images/Photolibrary; 19, © Juniors Bildarchiv/Alamy; 20, © Dwight Kuhn/Dwight Kuhn Photography; 21, © Rob Nunnington/Oxford Scientific/Photolibrary; 22TL, © Jacqui Hurst/Corbis; 22TR, © ArteSub/Alamy; 22BL, © Andrew J. Martinez/Photo Researchers, Inc./Photolibrary; 22BR, © Andrew J. Martinez/Photo Researchers, Inc./Photolibrary; 22Spot, © Yellowj/Shutterstock; 23TL, © Jim Wehtje/Photodisc/Getty Images; 23TR, © Robert Maier/Animals Animals Earth Scenes/Photolibrary; 23BL, © ANT Photo Library/Photo Researchers, Inc.; 23BR, © Alan Henderson; 24L, © Laurent Dambies/Shutterstock; 24R, © crystalfoto/Shutterstock.

Publisher: Kenn Goin
Editorial Director: Adam Siegel
Creative Director: Spencer Brinker
Original Design: Dawn Beard Creative
Photo Researcher: Q2A Media: Farheen Aadil

Library of Congress Cataloging-in-Publication Data

White, Nancy, 1942–
  Creeping land snails / by Nancy White.
     p. cm. — (No backbone! The world of invertebrates)
  Includes bibliographical references and index.
  ISBN-13: 978-1-59716-753-6 (library binding)
  ISBN-10: 1-59716-753-3 (library binding)
  1. Snails—Juvenile literature. 2. Slugs (Mollusks)—Juvenile literature. I. Title.

  QL430.4.W49 2009
  594'.38—dc22

                                2008033509

For more information, write to Bearport Publishing Company, Inc., 101 Fifth Avenue, Suite 6R, New York, New York 10003. Printed in the United States of America.

10 9 8 7 6 5 4 3 2 1

Contents

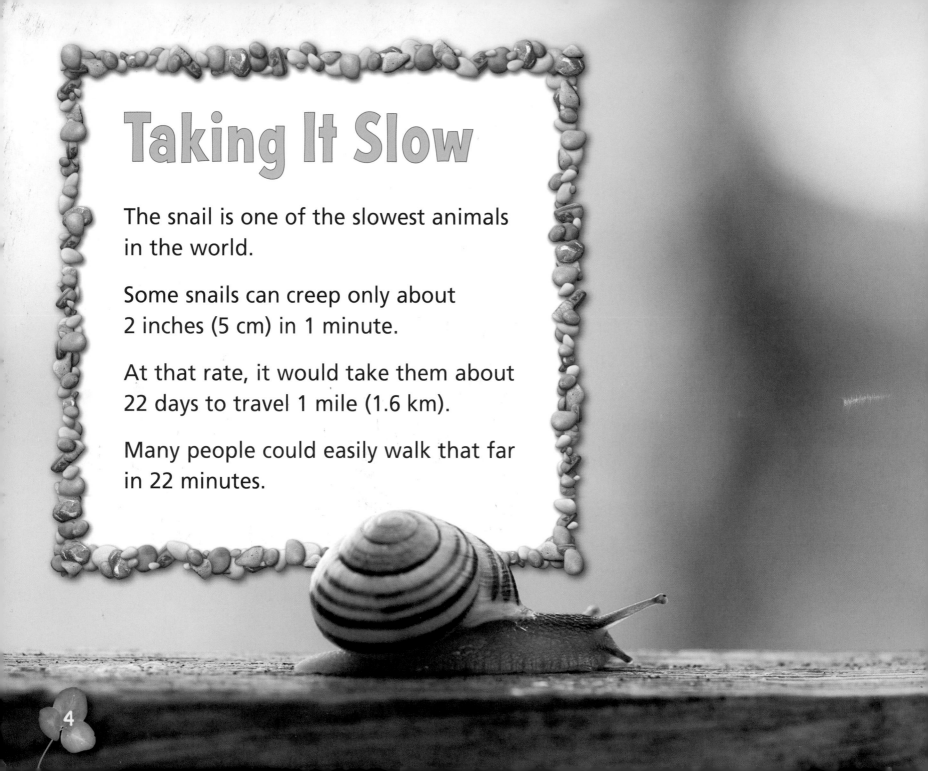

Taking It Slow

The snail is one of the slowest animals in the world.

Some snails can creep only about 2 inches (5 cm) in 1 minute.

At that rate, it would take them about 22 days to travel 1 mile (1.6 km).

Many people could easily walk that far in 22 minutes.

More than 30,000 kinds of snails live on land. Even more kinds live in oceans, lakes, ponds, and other bodies of water.

Heading Out

As a snail creeps slowly along, it carries its **shell** on its back.

The shell protects the animal's soft, boneless body.

The snail's head sticks out of an opening in the front of the shell.

On top of its head are two long **tentacles** with tiny eyes at the ends.

The snail can wave the tentacles around to see where it's going.

A snail's head also has two shorter tentacles. They are used for feeling and smelling.

long tentacles for seeing

short tentacles for feeling and smelling

6

One Big Foot

A snail has only one foot.

It is attached to the animal's head!

When a snail sticks its head out of its shell, its foot comes out, too.

The snail uses its foot to creep along the ground—very slowly.

The bottom of a snail's foot is called the *sole*—just like the bottom of a person's foot.

head

foot

9

Sliding on Slime

A snail can crawl over rocks, sticks, and logs.

How?

Its body makes a thick, slippery liquid called **slime**.

The slime makes it easy for the snail's foot to slide over rough objects.

As the snail creeps along, it leaves behind a silvery slime trail.

Slime isn't just slippery—it's sticky, too. A snail can climb up and down a tree or a plant stem without falling because its foot sticks to the gooey liquid.

slime

Don't Dry Out!

Land snails live in damp, shady spots like woods, leafy gardens, and piles of rocks.

They need to live in places like these because their bodies are made up mostly of water.

If they don't stay cool and moist, they will die.

A snail's slime helps keep its body from drying out.

13

Damp Dinners

Snails come out in damp, drizzly weather or at night to look for food.

They feed on grass, leaves, and mushrooms.

They like to eat lettuce, cabbage, and spinach from vegetable gardens, too.

Some kinds of snails also eat tiny insects, worms, and other snails.

Inside a snail's mouth is a tongue-like part covered with thousands of tiny sharp teeth. A snail uses it like a saw to shred its food into tiny bits.

mushroom

15

A Long Sleep

Cold winter weather can freeze a snail's moist body.

A snail that lives in a place that gets cold has a way of surviving, however.

It pulls its head and foot into its shell.

It closes up the opening with slime, leaving just a small hole for air to breathe.

Then it sleeps inside until spring.

Snails live all over the world. Those that live in places with hot, dry summers close up their shells and sleep until cooler weather comes in the fall.

Hiding from Enemies

Shells are not just a place for snails to sleep in through bad weather.

Snails also use shells to hide from enemies.

Many kinds of animals hunt and eat snails.

Birds, frogs, beetles, snakes, and mice are just a few of them.

A snail tries to stay safe from these enemies by pulling its head and foot into its shell.

People in many countries think that soft, tender snails are a tasty dish, too. The snails are often cooked with garlic and butter.

A Shell for Life

Baby snails hatch from eggs.

Each baby snail already has a tiny shell when it comes out of its egg.

The shell will get bigger as the small animal grows.

The snail will always carry the shell on its back as it moves slowly through life.

snail eggs

snails hatching

baby snails

giant African snail

Some land snails are only as big as a grain of rice. Others, like the giant African snail, grow up to 15 inches (38 cm) long—that's bigger than this book!

21

A World of Invertebrates

An animal that has a skeleton with a **backbone** inside its body is a *vertebrate* (VUR-tuh-brit). Mammals, birds, fish, reptiles, and amphibians are all vertebrates.

An animal that does not have a skeleton with a backbone inside its body is an *invertebrate* (in-VUR-tuh-brit). More than 95 percent of all kinds of animals on Earth are invertebrates.

Some invertebrates, such as insects and spiders, have hard skeletons—called exoskeletons—on the outside of their bodies. Other invertebrates, such as worms and jellyfish, have soft, squishy bodies with no exoskeletons to protect them.

Here are four invertebrates that are closely related to snails. Like snails, each of them has a soft, boneless body and a hard shell. Unlike snails, each of these animals has a two-part shell that can open and close.

Pacific Oyster

Giant Clam

Blue Mussel

Bay Scallop

Glossary

backbone
(BAK-bohn)
a group of connected bones that run along the backs of some animals, such as dogs, cats, and fish; also called a spine

shell (SHEL)
a hard covering that protects some animals

slime (SLIME)
a sticky, slippery goo that a snail uses to help it move

tentacles
(TEN-tuh-kuhlz)
body parts that grow out of a snail's head and are used for seeing, feeling, and smelling

Index

Read More

Green, Jen. *Snails.* Danbury, CT: Grolier (2004).

Llewellyn, Claire, and Barrie Watts. *Slugs and Snails.* Danbury, CT: Franklin Watts (2002).

Learn More Online

To learn more about snails, visit

www.bearportpublishing.com/NoBackbone–CreepyCrawlers

About the Author

Nancy White has written many science and nature books for children. She lives with her husband and her cat in New York's Hudson River Valley.